INTERIOR SPACES OF EUROPE

VOLUME 2

A PICTORIAL REVIEW OF EUROPEAN INTERIORS

INTERIOR SPACES OF EUROPE

VOLUME 2

A PICTORIAL REVIEW OF EUROPEAN INTERIORS

ISBN 1 86470 010 6

The Images Publishing Group Pty Ltd
Melbourne, Australia 1999
Printed in Singapore

Contents

Commercial Space and Atria

Sybase Headquarters and Training Centre
Paris, France
STUDIOS Architecture

1 Custom designed desk echoes company logo
2 Ambulatory links projection room, break-out areas and meeting rooms
3 Conveniences are provided throughout Training Centre
4 Black diamond grid panel adds textural and visual interest

1

2

3

5

6

7

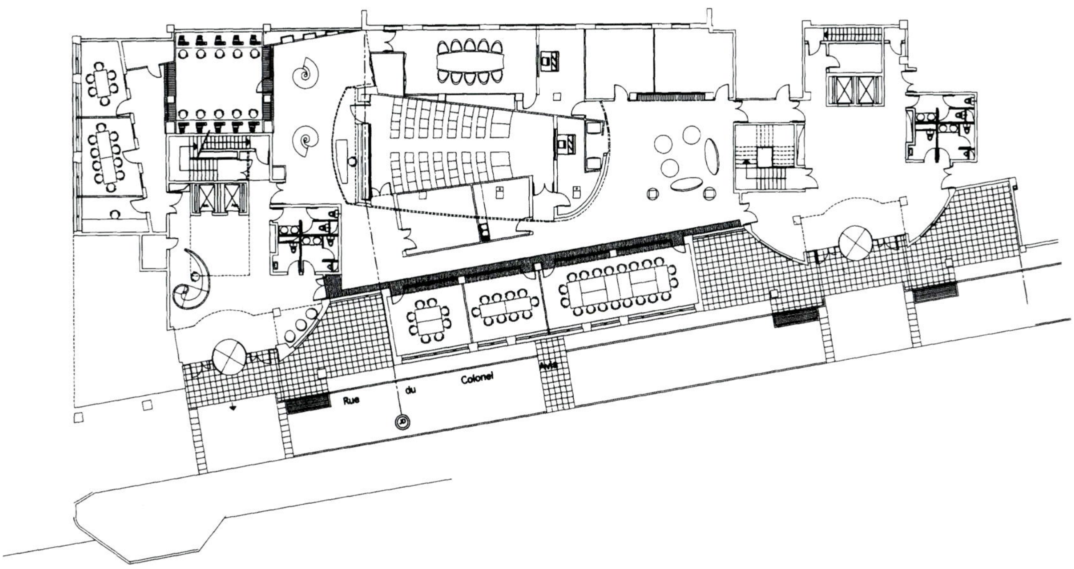

Sybase Headquarters and Training Centre
Paris, France
STUDIOS Architecture

5 Jewel-box showroom features product in display alcoves
6 Warm colours and curving walls in classroom break-out space
7 Break-out area
8 Floor plan of Training Centre

8

9

10

Sybase Headquarters and Training Centre
Paris, France
STUDIOS Architecture
9 Open office workstations
10 Dining area adjacent to first-floor classrooms
Opposite:
Small auditorium with rear-view projection system
Photo credit: Jean Philippe Caulliez

1

2

3

4

5

6

7

BP Presentation Suite
London, UK
Harper Mackay Architects

1 Space can act as single 150-seat auditorium or as clear reception space for 300 people
2 Suite can also be used as large meeting room with space for 32 people
3 Individual meeting spaces, each large enough for 12 people
4 Modern flexible conference space

Photo credit: Chris Gascoigne

Executive Office
Westminster, London, UK
Aukett Tytherleigh Interior Architects

5 Private meeting area
6 Reception

Photo credit: Dennis Gilbert

10 Dean Farrar Street
London, UK
Michael Squire and Partners, Architects

7 New entrance

Photo credit: Peter Cook/VIEW

Sabine MEUTER
Jean-Pierre LECHAT

Citibank Brussels
Brussels, Belgium
GMW Partnership
Open-plan workstations and atrium in Citibank's new European headquarters
Photo credit: Jeremy Cockayne

1

2

3

4

5

6

7

8

M & C Saatchi
Golden Square, London, UK
Harper Mackay Architects

1 Existing building is dynamic working environment that reinforces M & C Saatchi as leaders in world wide market
2 Reception leads to new atrium space which spirals upwards, incorporating floors above
3 Reception leads to café/informal meeting area

Photo credit: Chris Gascoigne

DDB Needham Worldwide
Paris, France
STUDIOS Architecture

4 Open reception area allows for informal meetings
5 Fluid floor plan accommodates clients and staff
6 Both clients and staff gather at curving coffee bar
7 Conference room

Photo credit: Jean Philippe Caulliez

Maghraj Bank Offices
London, UK
Jestico + Whiles Architects

8 Furnishings

Photo credit: Jo Reid and John Peck; Mrs Collingwood

1

2

3

4

5

Laboratories and Offices—CNRS of Grenoble
France
Herault-Arnod Architectes

1 Laboratory area
2 Meeting area
3 Mezzanine passage to offices and laboratories
4 Meeting and documentation rooms

Photo credit: André Morin

8 Cromwell Place
London, UK
Michael Squire and Partners, Architects

5 View of library

Opposite:
View of new linking stair

Photo credit: Peter Cook /VIEW

Photonics Centre
Berlin, Germany
sauerbruch hutton architects

1 Site plan
2&Opposite:
Production hall

1

2

SÜDSTAHL GmbH

5

6

7

Photonics Centre
Berlin, Germany
sauerbruch hutton architects
Opposite:
Entrance hall
5 Entrance hall detail, blinds down
Photo credit: Bitter Bredt Fotografte

Green Island
Brussels, Belgium
Atelier d'Art Urbain & Michel Jaspers
6 Entrance
7 Hall
Photo credit: Yvan Glavie

Conrad Ritblat
London, UK
GMW Partnership
Office reception area for Conrad Ritblat's London offices
Photo credit: Jeremy Cockayne

1

2

3

Secret Garden
Inca-Mallorca, Spain
Alberto Campo Baeza Arquitecto

1 Cafeteria, orange trees to left and patio corridor to right
2 Mountains are reflected in southeast corner
3 View from inside cafeteria, sun entering southwest corner

Photo credit: courtesy Alberto Campo Baeza Arquitecto

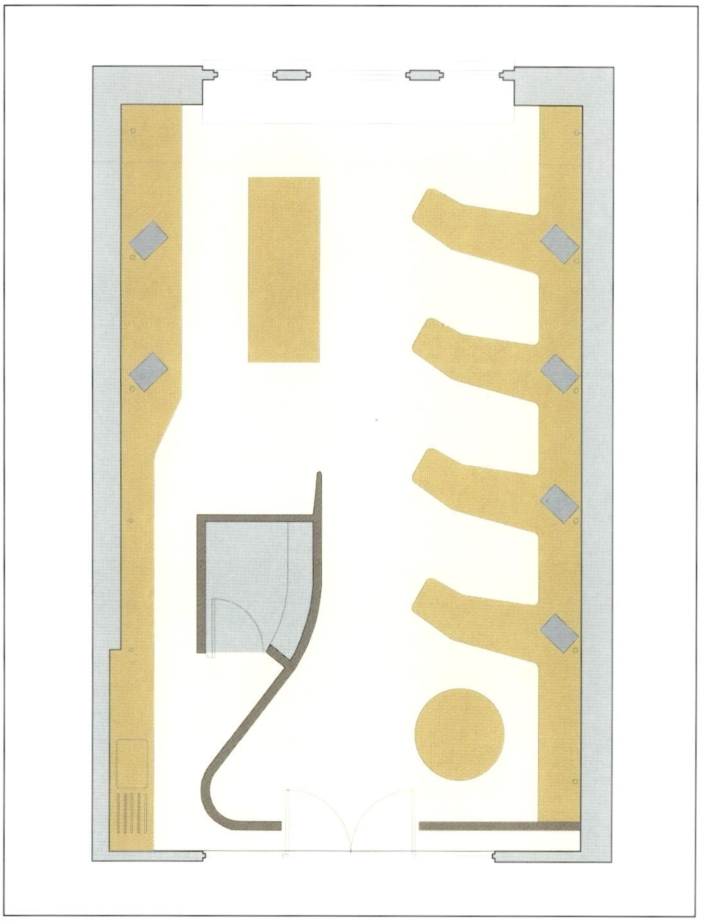
1

2

3

4

Chen Tsoi
Camden, London, UK
Tonkin Design

1 Plan
2 Workspace
3 Reception
4 Storage

Photo credit: courtesy Tonkin Design

ICAS PR Headquarters
Hemel Hempstead, UK
Jestico + Whiles Architects

5 Table detail

Photo credit: Paul Ratigan

Independiente Record Headquarters
London, UK
Jestico + Whiles Architects
Associate: John Wotton

6 View of upper level
7 View of lower level
8 Enclosed stair
9 Reception area

Photo credit: Paul Ratigan

5

6

7

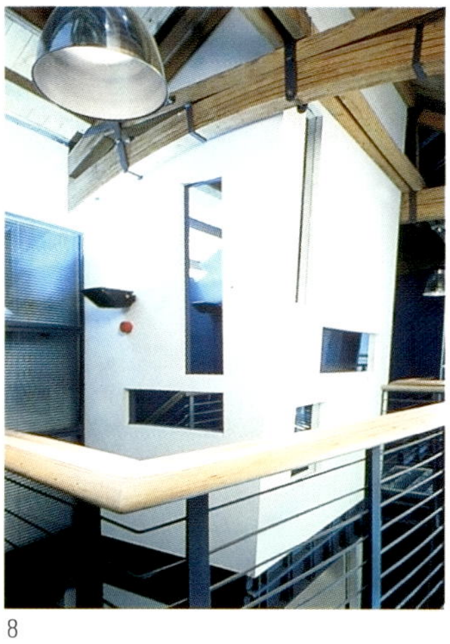

8

9

J. Walter Thompson
London, UK
Fletcher Priest Architects
1&2 Office area
Photo credit: Dennis Gilbert/VIEW

Executive Office
Southbank, London, UK
Aukett Tytherleigh Interior Architects
3 Open meeting area
4 Detail of Helical staircase
Photo credit: Dennis Gilbert

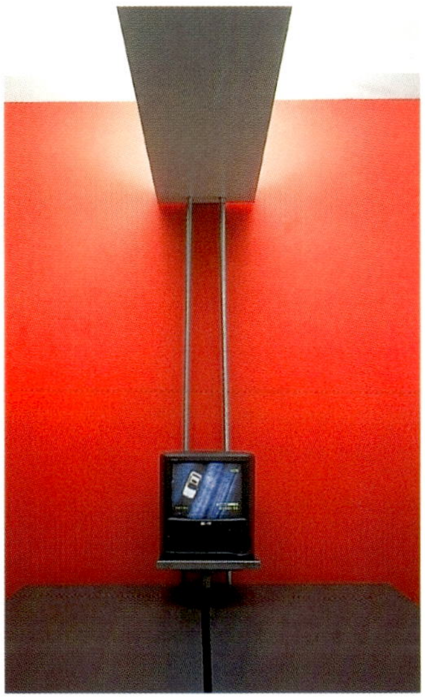
1

2

3

4

No1 Neathouse Place
London, UK
Avery Associates

1 Section
2 4–9th floors, office interior northeast side
3 Main stair

Photo credit: courtesy Avery Associates

Bartle Bogle Hegarty
London, UK
Fletcher Priest Architects

4 Stair, meeting cubes
5 Meeting cubes

Photo credit: Chris Caulfield-Dollard

99 Bishopgate for Hammerson plc
London, UK
GMW Partnership

6 Waiting area in main reception as part of total refurbishment of a 48,600-square-metre office building

Photo credit: Alan Williams

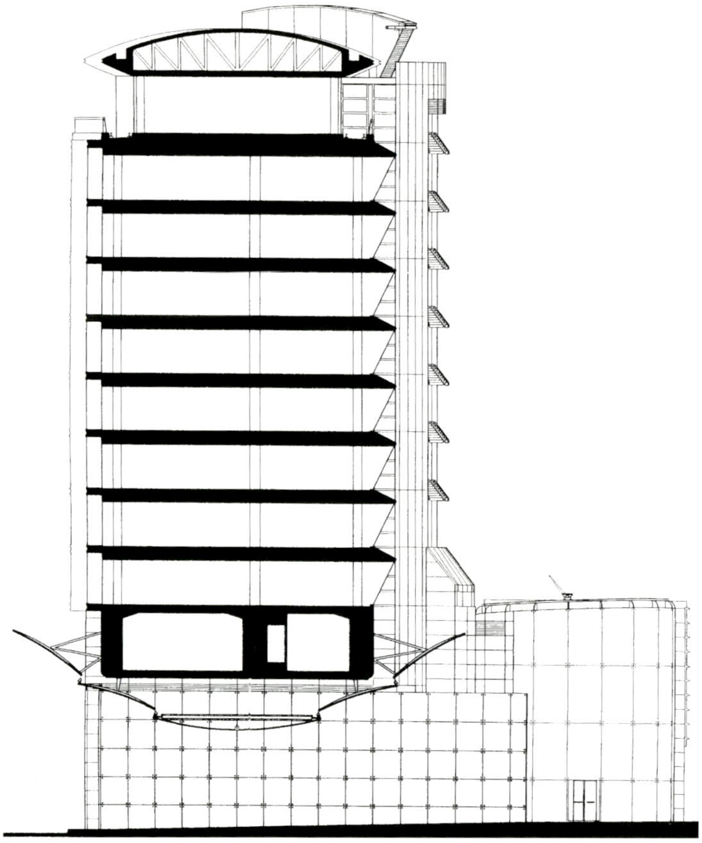
1

2

3

4

5

6

Greencoat House
London, UK
Michael Squire and Partners, Architects

1 Axonometric of new entrance works
2 View of reception with configured stair
3 Main stair

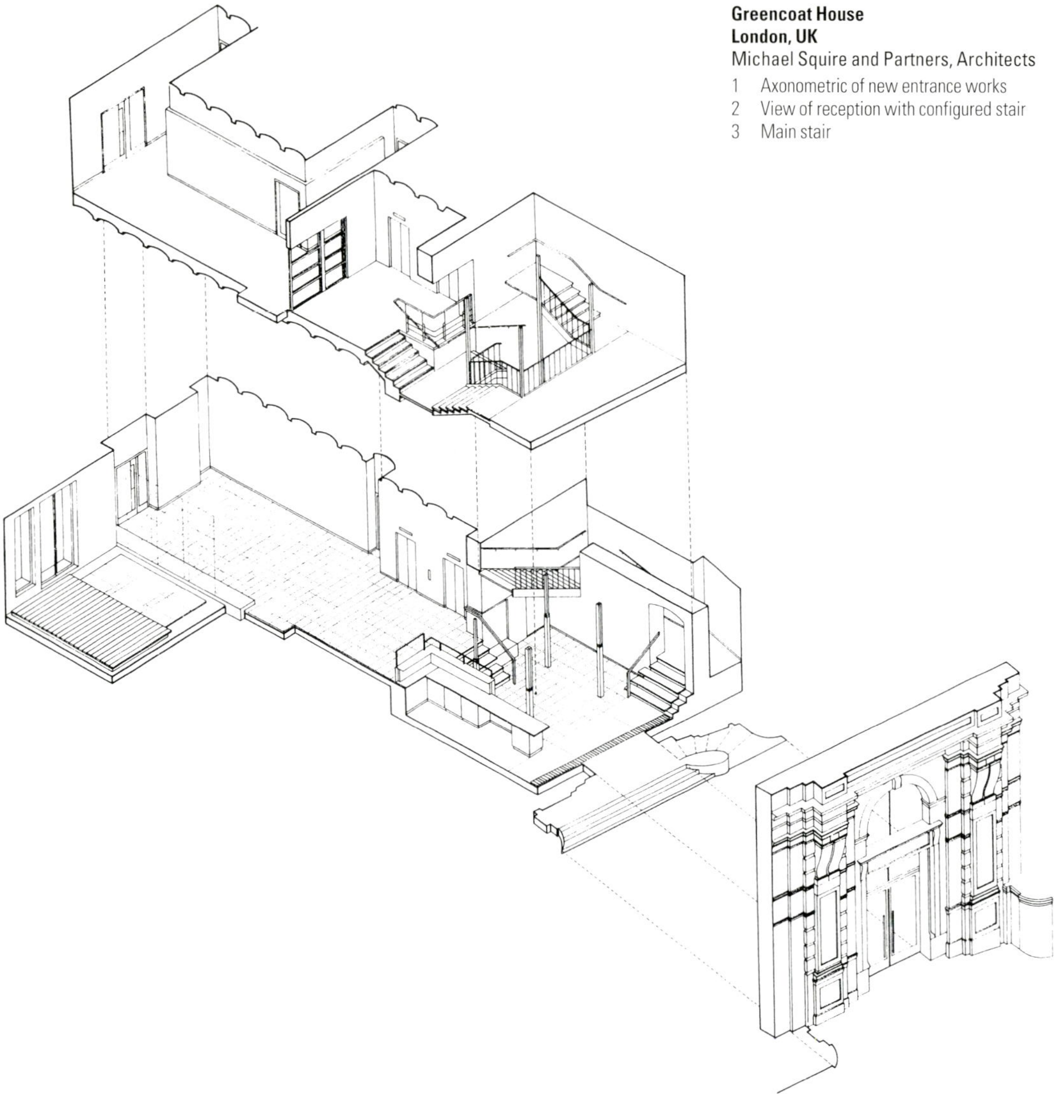

1

2

3

4

5

6

7

8

9

Greencoat House
London, UK
Michael Squire and Partners, Architects

4 Typical tenancy
5 Upper reception area
Photo credit: Peter Cook/VIEW

Ericsson Palac Office/Apartments
Prague, Czech Republic
Jestico + Whiles Architects

6 View of winter garden
7 Winter garden detail
8 Staircase to apartments
9 View from offices to winter garden
Photo credit: courtesy Jestico + Whiles Architects

2

Headquarters Building
Slough Estates, London, UK
Michael Aukett Architects
with Aukett Tytherleigh Interior Architects

Previous pages:
Casual meeting area
2 Open office plan
3 View from reception desk
Photo credit: Dennis Gilbert

3

2

3

Eva-Company
Reykjavík, Iceland
Studio Granda

Opposite:
In situ concrete court facade with pigtail bolthole plugs
2 New retail space between two planes of concrete, one honed, one sand-blasted
3 View of courtyard from street
Photo credit: Sigurgeir Sigurjónsson

2

3

4

Aston Chase Offices
London, UK
Blauel Architects

Opposite:
Basement, stairs with steel chain-mail blind
2 Offices with stairs and steel chain-mail blind
3 Detail of stairs and steel chain-mail blind
4 Glazed office
Following pages:
Offices
Photo credit: Dennis Gilbert/VIEW

1

3

2

4

5

Apple Showroom
Nantes, France
Odile Decq and Benoit Cornette

1 Demonstration points on pivoting wing partitions
2 Pivoting partitions of meeting rooms
3 Pivoting wing partitions in aluminium
4 Library in office area
5 View of meeting room from entrance

Photo credit: Philippe Ruault

Silicon Graphics Computer Systems
Cortaillod, Switzerland
STUDIOS Architecture

6 Circulation link
7 Circulation arcade with glass skylight separates offices from factory
8 Natural light floods entire volume of lobby area
9 Vertical circulation connected to mezzanine balcony
10 View of upper mezzanine
11 Stairs to upper levels float around massive concrete pillar

Photo credit: STUDIOS Architecture (6,10); Paul Warchol (7,8,11); Fausto Pluchinotta (9)

6

7

8

9

10

11

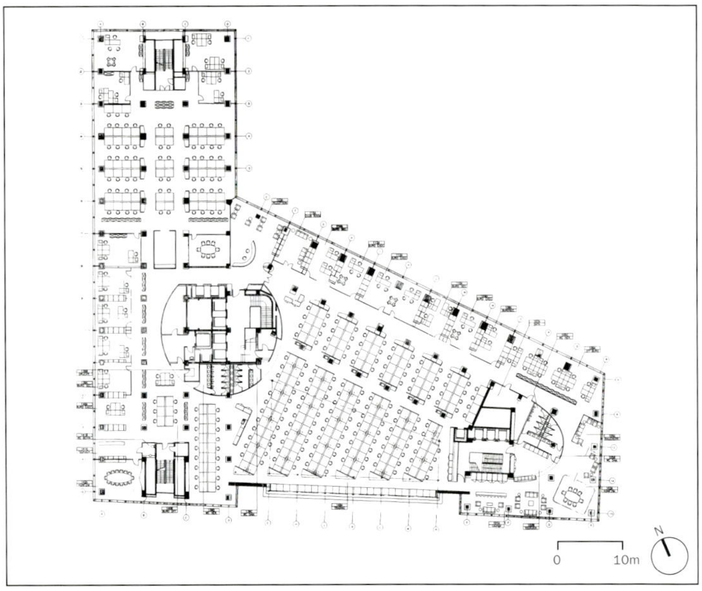

1

2

3

4

5

6

Bankgesellschaft Berlin
Berlin, Germany
STUDIOS Architecture

1 Floor plan
2&3 Trading floor
4 Open plan creates informal gathering points

Photo credit: Christian Kerber (2,4); Michael O'Callahan Photography (3)

Charterhouse Mews
London, UK
Avery Associates

5 Conference room interior
6 Office interior

Photo credit: courtesy Avery Associates

7

8

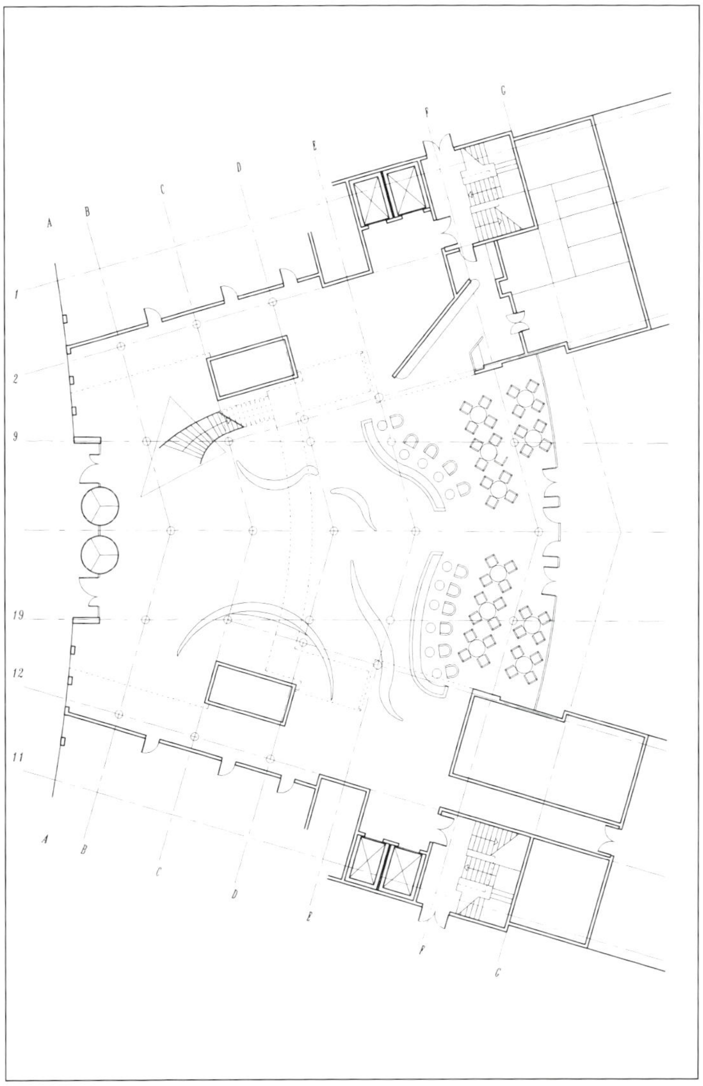

9

10

11

12

13

Spreebogen Plaza
Berlin, Germany
STUDIOS Architecture

7 Cherry wood benches slither around columns
8 Bench backs designed to create privacy between diners and lobby
9 Floor plan

Photo credit: Michael O'Callahan Photography

The Benfield Group
London, UK
Austin-Smith: Lord

10 Reception
11 Glazed wall and reception area
12 Staff restaurant
13 Meeting room

Photo credit: Nick Hufton

Pfizer Building 550
Kent, UK
GMW Partnership
Office reception area of Pfizer Building 550 which provides 11,000 m2 of offices
Photo credit: Jeremy Cockayne

Palais Equitable—Vienna 1, Stock im Eisen Platz 3
Vienna, Austria
Architect Prof. Rüdiger Lainer

1 Light-wall by Michael Kienzer
2 View along middle wall
3 View along main entrance from interior

Photo credit: Margherita Spiluttini

France Television Headquarters
Paris, France
Jean-Paul Viguier S.A. d'Architecture

4 Catwalk
5 Grand lobby

Photo credit: Georges Fessy Photograph, courtesy Jean-Paul Viguier S.A. d'Architecture

1

2

4

3

5

Grand Duchy of Luxembourg Diplomatic Missions
Brussels, Belgium
Bureau d'Architecture Henri Montois and Théo Worré

1 Entrance hall
2 Grand staircase to mezzanine
3 Lobby of the Ambassador
4 Mezzanine

Photo credit: Marc Detiffe, courtesy Bureau d'Architecture Henri Montois

1

2

3

4

2

3

Gerling Insurance
Germany
gmp-von Gerkan, Marg & Partners
Opposite:
One of three identical entrance halls, building is acoustically sheltered from street
2 Lightweight design of internal stairs
Photo credit: courtesy gmp-von Gerkan, Marg & Partners

Hogeschool voor de Kunsten Art Academy
Arhem, Netherlands
Hubert-Jan Henket architecten bna
3 Glass bridge interior
Photo credit: van der Vlugt & Claus

1

2

Generale Bank Tower
Rotterdam, The Netherlands
Murphy/Jahn

1 Auto-ramp drop off
2 Lobby/reception

1

2

3

4

5

6

Radison SAS Hotel
Brussels, Belgium
Michel Jaspers & Atelier d'Art Urbain

1 Atrium

Photo credit: Serge Brison

Kredietbank
Brussels, Belgium
Michel Jaspers & Atelier d'Art Urbain

2 Atrium

Photo credit: Serge Brison

T'Hoofd-Seghers Engineering
Brussels, Belgium
Samyn and Partners

3 Glazed openings and white plain surfaces conduct light to bottom of atrium
4 Nearby clock tower is glimpsed when ascending stairs
5 Natural light floods stairwell
6 Circular axis of staircase
7 Floodlit spiral staircase
8 View of spiral staircase and elevator, looking up
9 Opposite spiral staircase in atrium, is transparent elevator

7

8

9

10

12

11

13

14

T'Hoofd-Seghers Engineering
Brussels, Belgium
Samyn and Partners

10 Aesthetically designed functional office furniture
11 Atrium blends fluidly with office area
12 Circles and squares punctuate space in meeting room
13 Windows provide views of brick facade of old brewery
14 Mirrors allow natural light to penetrate deeply within building

Photo credit: Jan Verlinden

1

2

3

4

Levis' European Headquarters
Brussels, Belgium
Samyn and Partners

1 Metallic grid partition allows natural light within staricase
2 Vertical metallic grid provides a secure railing
3 Metallic grids on ceiling are associated with light sources
4 Spacious amphitheatre is enhanced with simple and efficient materials and fixtures

5

6

7

8

Levis' European Headquarters
Brussels, Belgium
Samyn and Partners

5 Simple flooring and ceiling materials provide flexible display area
6 Glazed panels on elevator allow view through entrance courtyard
7 Columns and braces are discreet but essential components of space
8 Horizontal stripes in glazed louvres on transparent elevator

Photo credit: Fabien de Cugnac

Adam Opel Headquarters
Rüsselsheim, Germany
BDP

1 Atrium, with reception at ground floor and café on first floor
2 Cascade of escalators
3 View of atrium across landscaped lake, with cars on display islands

Photo credit: Dennis Gilbert

1

2

3

2

3

4

5

6

7

Hochhaus RWE AG Konzernzentrale Essen
Essen, Germany
Ingenhoven Overdiek Kahlen und Partner

Previous page:
Open stairs in upper floors
2 Entrance
3 Lobby
4 Each floor is opened up by free-standing lift tower
5 Entrance hall
6 Part of entrance hall
7 Conference room

8

Hochhaus RWE AG Konzernzentrale Essen
Essen, Germany
Ingenhoven Overdiek Kahlen und Partner

8 Meeting/conference room
9 Entrance, typical office
10 Multi-functional ceiling element/facade

Photo credit: Holger Knauf

9

10

1

2

3

Lintas, Advertising Agency Offices
Brussels, Belgium
ASSAR/GLOBAL
1 Atrium and stair
Photo credit: Marc Detiffe

LWWK, Lawyers Offices
Brussels, Belgium
ASSAR/GLOBAL
2 Atrium
Photo credit: Marc Detiffe

GFK Offices
Brussels, Belgium
ASSAR/GLOBAL
3 Entry hall and reception desk
Photo credit: Marc Detiffe

SCOTTISH WIDOWS

2

Scottish Widows Headquarters
Port Hamilton, Edinburgh, Scotland, UK
BDP

Opposite:
Broad stairway leading to atrium
2 View of atrium from bridge link
Following pages:
Atrium at dusk

4

Scottish Widows Headquarters
Port Hamilton, Edinburgh, Scotland, UK
BDP
4 Boardroom level with view of Edinburgh Castle
Photo credit: Keith Hunter

1

2

3

4

5

AXA Belgium, Insurance Company Headquarters Building
Brussels, Belgium
ASSAR with Jean Claude De Wever

1 Executive office level
2–4 Entry hall
Photo credit: Marc Detiffe

Seed Factory, Offices in Renovated Industrial Hall
Brussels, Belgium
ASSAR/GLOBAL

5 Entry hall with stair
Photo credit: Marc Detiffe

NOE
LOBB

2

Marriott County Hall
London, UK
RPW Interior Design Consultants
1 'Noes Lobby'
2 Leader's Bar

Marriott County Hall
London, UK
RPW Interior Design Consultants
3 Public area corridor
4 County Hall Restaurant
Opposite:
Library
Photo credit: courtesy RPW Interior Design Consultants

3

4

1

2

Fitzwilliam Hotel
Dublin, Republic of Ireland
CD Partnership

1&4 Bar
2 Detail, niche entrance
3 Entrance foyer

Photo credit: Denis Mortell

4

1

2

Bertorelli's
London, UK
Harper Mackay Architects

1 New glazed oak doors open on to terrace of oak duckboarding, with space for eating out in summer

2 Old atrium has been moved to back of building where it takes natural light

Opposite:
Broad shallow flight of Palazzo-style stairs honed with limestone treads, with glass balustrading, leads to main restaurant

Following pages:
Bar counters are made of Calcutta-Vaggli Rosata marble

5

6

Bertorelli's
London, UK
Harper Mackay Architects

5 Woven lattice of veneered plywood, strips of marble and American black oak, inset with brightly coloured display boxes stocked with ceramics
6 Pivoting oak faced doors to cubicles, imperial single-unit sink made from angled slab of Calcutta-Vaggli Rosata marble

Photo credit: Nicholas Kane

1

2

3

4

5

6

7

8

9

Johan Restaurant
Graz, Austria
Architect Claudio Silvestrin
1–3 Restaurant seating area
4 Bar area
Photo credit: courtesy Architect Claudio Silvestrin

Scotts Bar & Restaurant
Cardiff, Wales, UK
Austin-Smith:Lord
5 Ground floor bar
6 Upstairs bar
Photo credit: Alan Williams

Marylebone Shop, 'The Orrery' restaurant
London, UK
CD Partnership
7 Restaurant
Photo credit: Peter Cook

Cafe Flo
Ludgate Hill, London UK
Jestico + Whiles Architects
Associate: Tony Ling
8 View of bar and screen
9 General view
Photo credit: Paul Ratigan

1

Cafe Flo
Haymarket, London UK
Jestico + Whiles Architects
Associate: Tony Ling

1 General view
2 View across front room
Photo credit: Paul Ratigan

2

1

First Choice Holidays
London Gatwick Airport, West Sussex, UK
GMW Partnership

1 Staff restaurant; part of the fitout of First Choice Holidays' UK headquarters

Photo credit: Jeremy Cockayne

1

2

3

4

Key:
1 Restaurant
2 Void over entrance
3 Function room
4 Terrace
5 Dispense bar
6 Open kitchen
7 Brewery
8 Void
9 Toilets
10 Stair

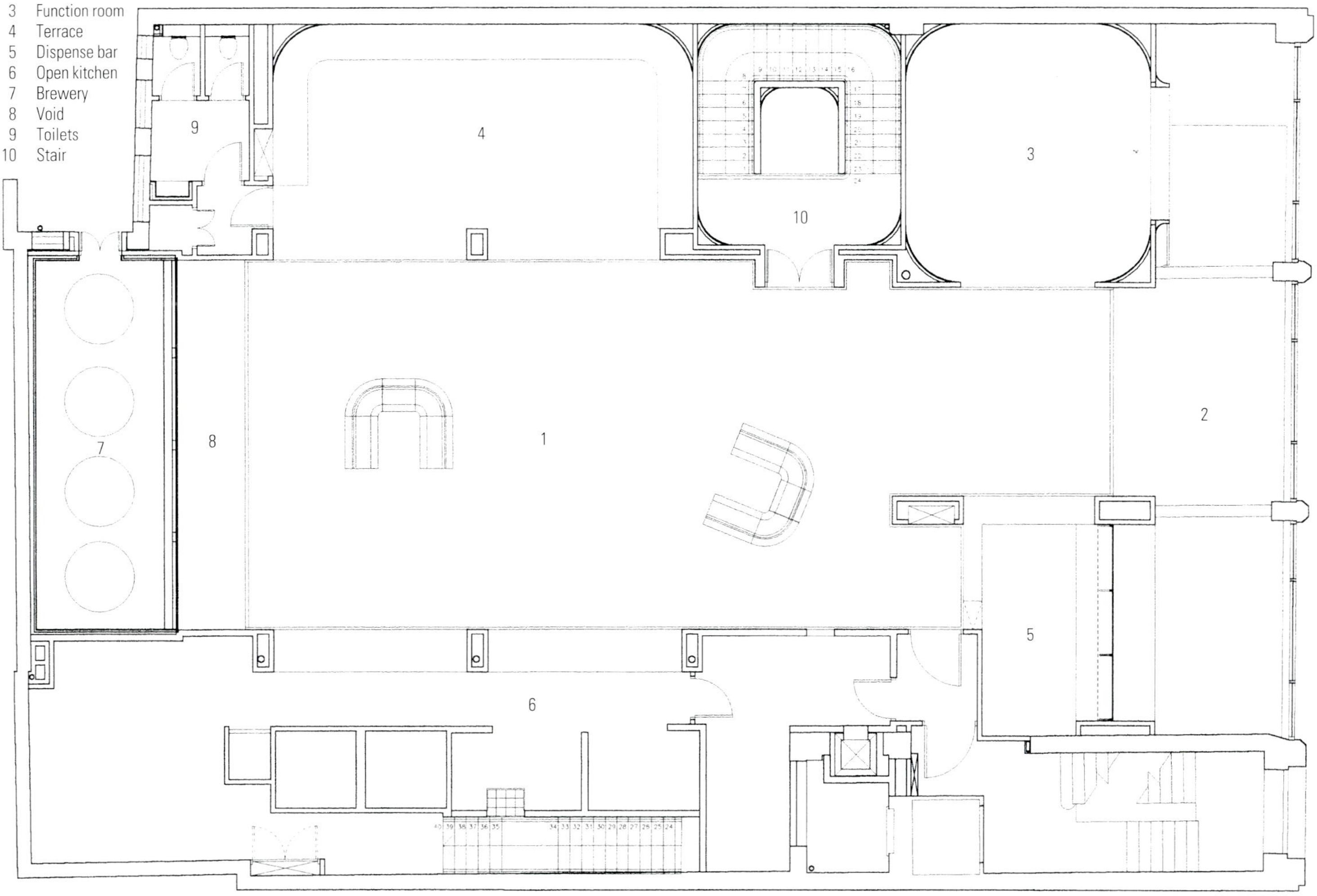

5

6

Harvey Nichols Restaurant
Leeds, UK
Hosker Moore & Kent

1 View of restaurant
2 View of restaurant bar

Photo credit: courtesy Hosker Moore & Kent

Mash 2
London, UK
Fin Architects and Designers

3 View into bar from entrance lobby
4 Entrance lobby
5 First floor plan
6 Function room

Photo credit: Larry Dunstan

Deli Bar
Naturally Sweet
Catch of the Day
Traditional Fare

Pfizer Building 550
Kent, UK
GMW Partnership
Restaurant and servery
Photo credit: Jeremy Cockayne

1

2

Victoria and Albert Museum
London, UK
Austin-Smith:Lord

1 Staff restaurant
2 Staff restaurant with screen by Wendy Ramshaw

Opposite:
Staff restaurant and seating area

Photo credit: Alan Williams

Please place your trays on the racks
Please place your trays on the racks

Crowne Plaza
Brussels, Belgium
Atelier d'Architecture de Genval
with Houben Design

1 Lobby foyer, reception area on right
2 Le Temps Présent restaurant
3 Derby bar
4 Ballroom

Photo credit: Marc Detiffe

1

2

3

4

Castle View Cafe
St Helier, Channel, France
Alsop and Stormer
1&Opposite:
Internal view
Photo credit: Roderick Coyne

Hochhaus RWE AG Konzernzentrale Essen
Essen, Germany
Ingenhoven Overdiek Kahlen und Partner
Following pages:
Ground floor restaurant
Photo credit: Holger Knauf

1

1

Halifax Headquarters
Halifax, Yorkshire, UK
BDP

1 Ground floor café
Photo credit: Martine Hamilton-Knight

Bus Centre Laganside
Belfast, Northern Ireland
BDP

2 Interior bus centre
Photo credit: Christopher Hill

2

1

2

3

Broadgate Health Club
London, UK
Allford Hall Monaghan Morris Architects

1 Entrance
2 External view of multi-coloured wall
3 External view of blue wall
4 Internal view of blue wall

4

5

6

Broadgate Health Club
London, UK
Allford Hall Monaghan Morris Architects
5&6 Gym
7 Changing room
Photo credit: Richard Bryant/ARCAID

7

Sackler Galleries, Royal Academy of Arts
Piccadilly, London, UK
Foster and Partners

1 Cutaway sketch by Sir Norman Foster
2 First floor lift lobby
3 Sculpture shelf and Michelangelo's Tondo

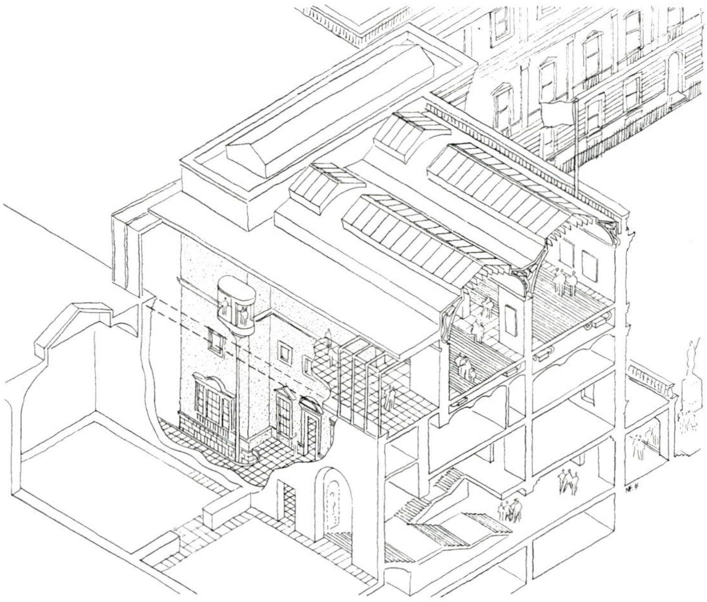

1

2

3

Sackler Galleries, Royal Academy of Arts
Piccadilly, London, UK
Foster and Partners

4 Glass staircase
Opposite:
Sculpture shelf

4

6

7

8

9

Sackler Galleries, Royal Academy of Arts
Piccadilly, London, UK
Foster and Partners

6 Interior view of galleries

Photo credit: Dennis Gilbert

Screen Cinema
Winchester, UK
Fletcher Priest Architects

7 Auditorium

Photo credit: Graham Challifour

Sony Pictures European Headquarters
London, UK
Fletcher Priest Architects

8 Stair detail
9 Screening room
10 View looking up atrium

Photo credit: Timothy Soar

10

1

2

3

4

5

6

7

8

9

10

CentrO Oberhausen
Oberhausen, Düsseldorf, Germany
RTKL International Ltd

1 Centre court atrium
2 Centre court skylight
3 Terrazzo floor design
4 CentrO interior
5 Handrail glass detail
6 Warner Bros. cinema interior

Photo credit: David Whitcomb (1–5); Photogenics (6)

Michael Hue Williams Gallery
London, UK
John Pawson

7 Gallery library
8 Gallery office
9 Gallery
10 View of entrance from gallery

Photo credit: Richard Glover

1

2

Eagle Pub
London, UK
Alsop and Stormer
1&2 Interior view
Photo credit: Roderick Coyne

Eureka! The Children's Museum
Halifax, Yorkshire, UK
BDP
Opposite:
Archimedes in his bath
Photo credit: Jonty Wilde

EUREKA!

1

2

3

Eureka! The Children's Museum
Halifax, Yorkshire, UK
BDP

Opposite:
Glazed entrance elevation
Photo credit: Rupert Truman

Leisure Swimming Pool
Sheringham, UK
Alsop and Stormer

1 View of slide
2 View of changing cabins
3 Internal view

Photo credit: Roderick Coyne

Teylers Museum
Haalem, The Netherlands
Hubert-Jan Henket architecten bna

Opposite:
'Oval Room' in main museum
2 Glazed passage between old museum and new exhibition hall

2

3

4

Teylers Museum
Haalem, The Netherlands
Hubert-Jan Henket architecten bna

3 Link between new building and old museum
4 Museum cafe

Photo credit: Martin Zegel (Previous page left); Sybolt Voeten (2–4)

The Music School
Stuttgart, Germany
Michael Wilford and Partners Limited

1 Section
2 Library
Opposite:
500-seat concert hall
Photo credit: Richard Bryant/ARCAID

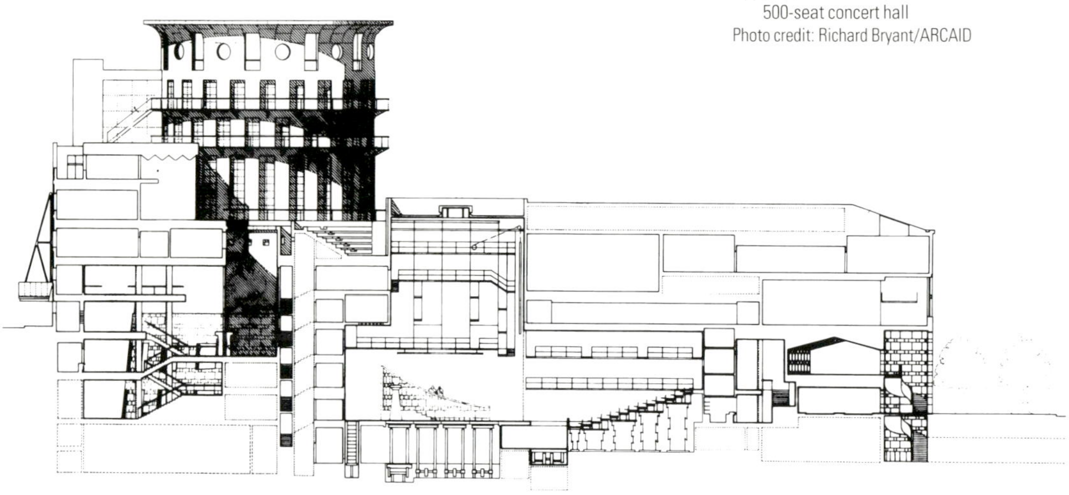

1

2

Earth Galleries Redevelopment, Natural History Museum
London, UK
Pawson Williams Architects

1 Section drawing through foyer gallery and perspectives
2 RTZ atrium from entrance foyer
3 Foyer gallery

Opposite:
Remodelled west stair

Following pages:
Foyer gallery detail

Photo credit: Nathan Willock

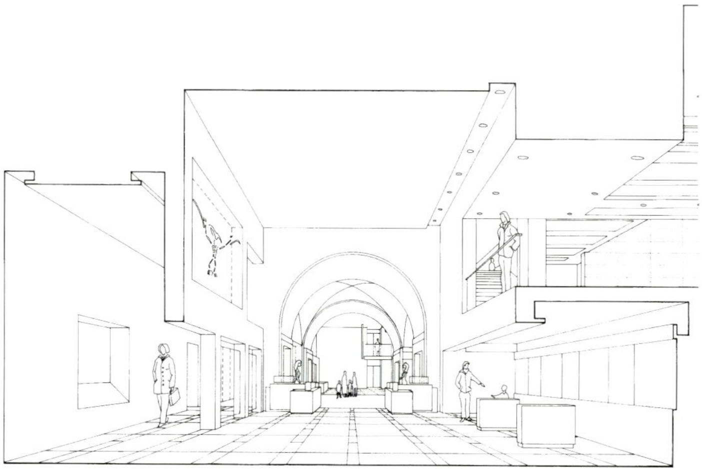
1

2

3

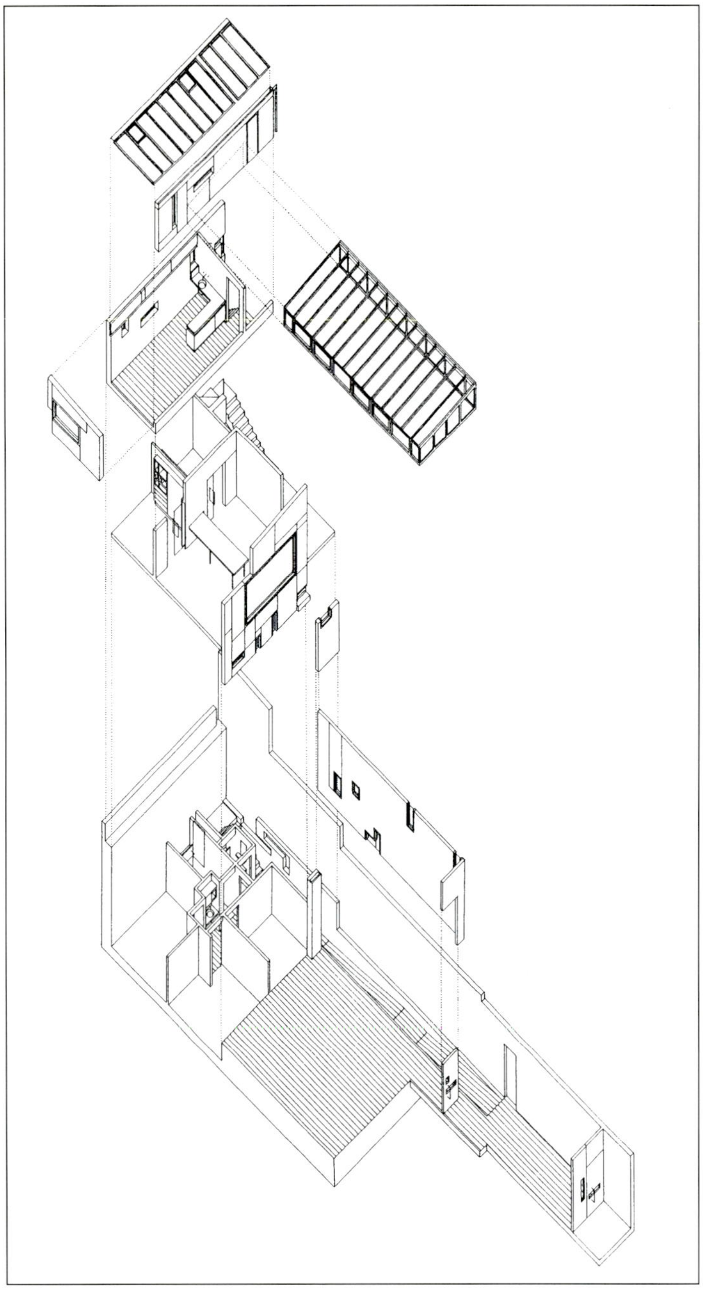

1

2

3

4

Film Production Studios
Mile End, London, UK
ECD Architects

1 Axonometric
2 View of ramped entrance corridor
3 Rooftop relaxation area
4 Toplit rehearsal room

Photo credit: Nicholas Kane

Gallery of 'Amphitheatres'—
Saint-Martin-D'Héres
France
Herault-Arnod Architectes

5 Cafeteria
6 Restored patio and facade
7 Main hall, restored area

Photo credit: André Morin

Information Point of Turin's Public
Transport
Italy
Sergio Jaretti Sodano Architetto

8 Hall with tram seats and section of tram front
9 View of assembly room with window screening
10 Hall, information desk with transport plan of city and section of tram front

Photo credit: Enzo Ricci

5

6

7

8

9

10

Kauniala Disabled War Veterans' Hospital
Renovation of Wards
Kauniainen, Finland
Paatela & Paatela Architects

1 Corridor detail
2 Dining
3 Kitchen
4&5 Lounge
6 Lobby

Photo credit: Timo Kauppi

2

1

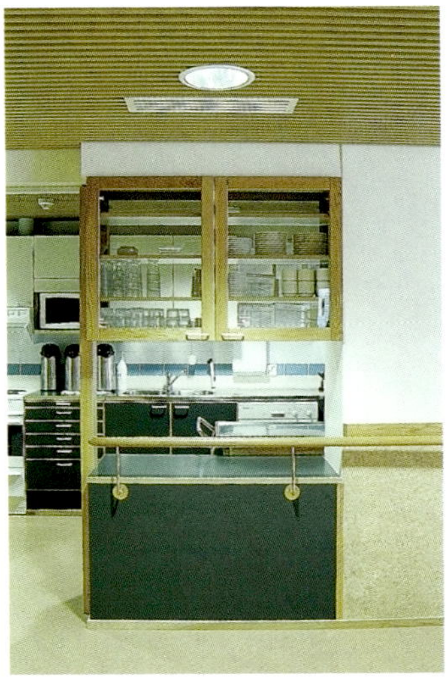

3

4

5

6

Limehouse Youth Club
London, UK
Michael Squire and Partners, Architects
7 View of art rooms from main hall
8 Axonometric
9 View of main hall towards climbing wall
Photo credit: Peter Cook/VIEW

7

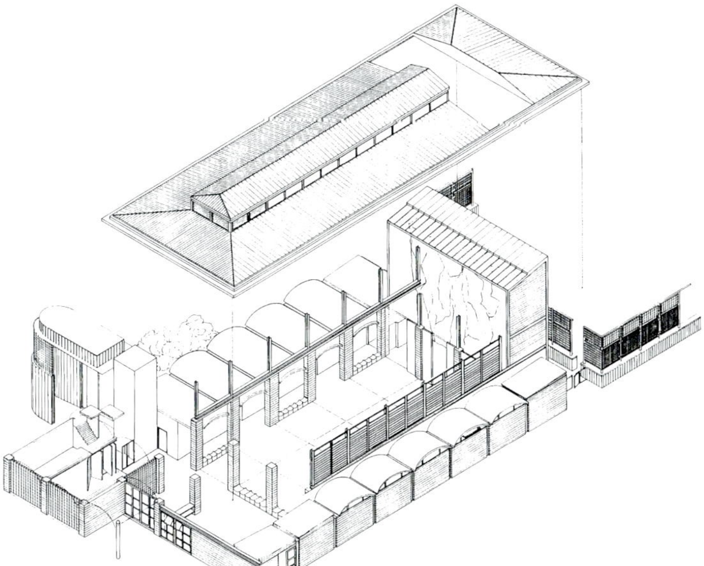

8

9

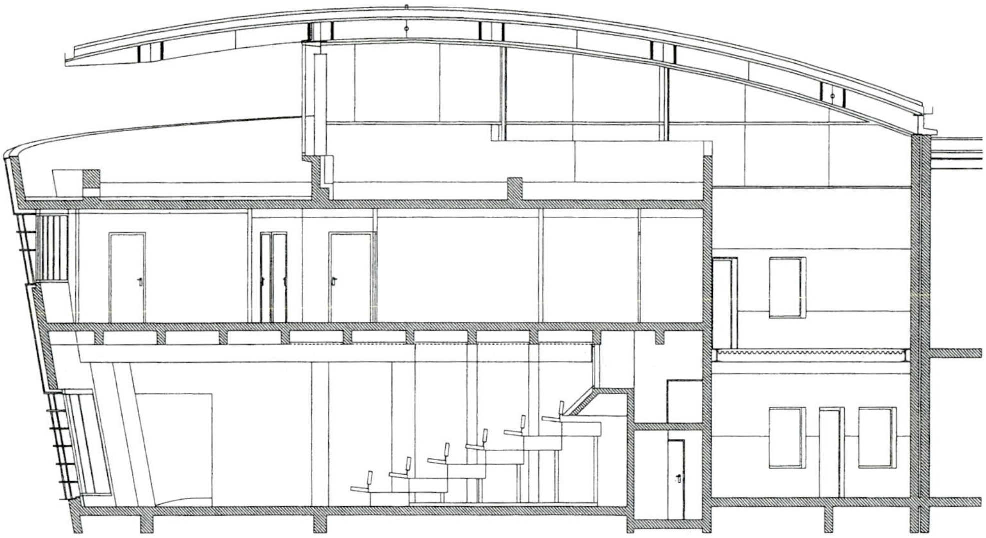

1

2

3

4

5

Morestel High School
France
Herault-Arnod Architectes

1 Administration section
2 Passage to classrooms
3 View of main hall from patio
4 Main hall, management and administration area
5 Main hall, library area

Photo credit: Georges Fessy

Primary School of Lozanne
France
Herault-Arnod Architectes

6 Longitudinal section
7 Main hall
8 Passage with alternate use of natural and artificial lights

Photo credit: André Morin

Rijksmuseum Twente
Enschede, The Netherlands
Van Berkel & Bos

9 View of exhibition hall

Following pages:
Exhibition hall detail

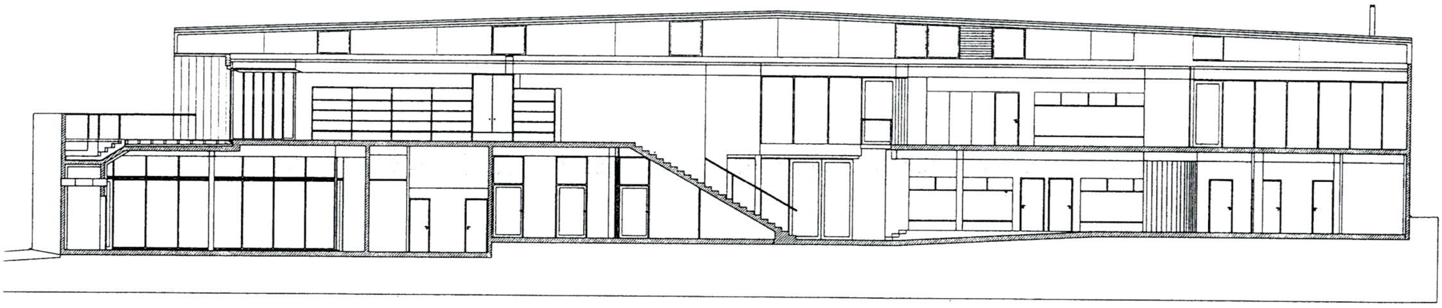

6

7

8

9

Rijksmuseum Twente
Enschede, The Netherlands
Van Berkel & Bos
11&12 Exhibition hall
Photo credit: Christian Richters Fotograf

11

12

2

Strandschool
Tyresoe, Sweden
Holm Arkitektkontor

Opposite:
Upper main corridor to northeast
2 Communication in learning area
Following pages:
Part of general learning area
Photo credit: Åke Eison Lindman

8

9

Hat Hill Sculpture Foundation
West Sussex, UK
StudioDownie

7 Central roof light, looking east into copse
8 Interior night view
9 Display space and gallery
Photo credit: Peter Cook

Plas Mawr
Conway, North Wales, UK
BDP

1 Restored roof beams
2 Decorative plasterwork in great chamber
Photo credit: Paul Highnam/CADW Welsh Historic Monuments

St Peters Campus, University of Sunderland, Phases I & II
Monkwearmouth, Sunderland, UK
BDP

3 Internal street, computer hall
Photo credit: Martine Hamilton-Knight

1

2

3

The Church of St Lucy (Chiesa di Santa Lucia)
Gemona, Udine, Italy
Burelli E Gennaro Architetti

Opposite&2
Main hall
Photo credit: Carlo Valsecchi

2

1

Ferry Terminal
Hamburg, Germany
Alsop and Stormer

1 View of city from top office
2 Internal view of terminal

Photo credit: Roderick Coyne

2

1

2

Hotel du Department des Bouches-du-Rhone
Marseilles, France
Alsop and Stormer

1 Entrance to press room in atrium
2 Front elevation of press room in atrium

4

Hotel du Department des Bouches-du-Rhone
Marseilles, France
Alsop and Stormer

Opposite:
Press room elevation
4 View of atrium
Photo credit: Roderick Coyne

Alexander Nicolette Shoe Store
Milano, Via Montenapoleone, Italy
Architetto Aurelio Cortesi

1 Floor plans
2 View of showroom
3 View of mezzanine from below

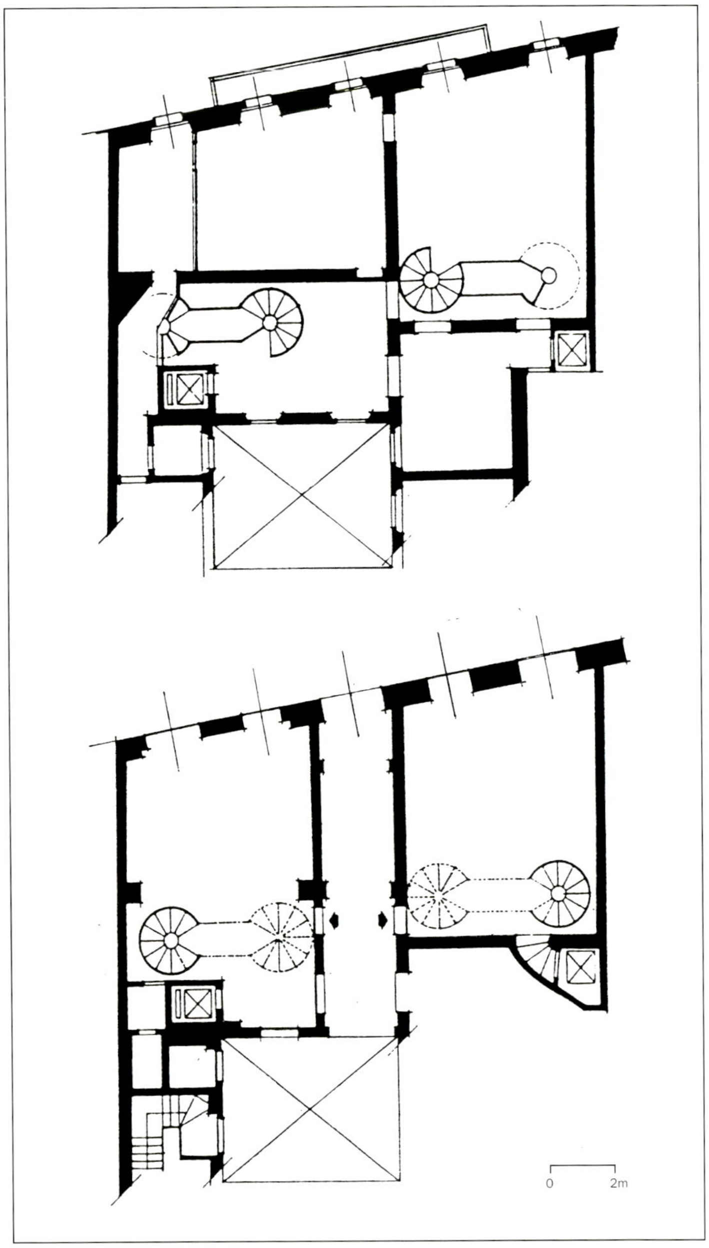

1

2

3

Alexander Nicolette Shoe Store
Milano, Via Montenapoleone, Italy
Architetto Aurelio Cortesi

4 View of staircase
5 View of mezzanine from above
6 Entrance to staircase from showroom
7 Detail of staircase from mezzanine
8 View of showroom
Opposite:
Ground floor, selling area
Photo credit: Dida Biggi, Katia Guglielmi

4

7

5

6

8

Angelo Fabbri Mall
Ravenna, Italy
Bruno Minardi with L. Zaganelli, M. Rossi & E. Brunetti

1 View from main gallery
2 Entrance to Mall in Grand Hall
3 New shops are partitioned by glass and white painted iron

1

2

3

5

6

Angelo Fabbri Mall
Ravenna, Italy
Bruno Minardi with L. Zaganelli, M. Rossi & E. Brunetti

Opposite:
Connection between old cast-iron columns and the new glass-iron partitions
5 Mall
6 Upper gallery
Photo credit: Marco Buzzoni

Calvin Klein Collection Store
Avenue Montaigne, Paris, France
Architect Claudio Silvestrin

1–3 Ground floor ladies' wear
4&5 First floor home collection

Photo credit: courtesy Calvin Klein Collection

Conran Collection Shop
London, UK
CD Partnership

6 Ground floor
7 Entrance
8 Basement floor

Photo credit: Georgia Glynn-Smith

Galleri
Reykjavík, Iceland
Studio Granda

9 Main shop with broad Tennessee maple boards. Changing rooms are in blue-grey column

1

2

3

4

5

6

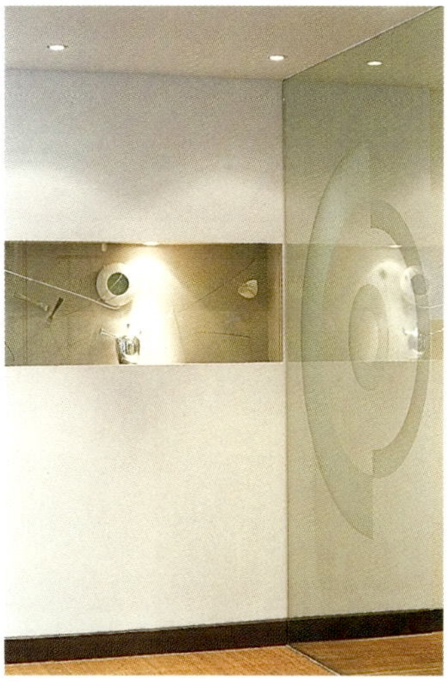
7

8

9

Galleri
Reykjavík, Iceland
Studio Granda
10&11 Service desk
12 Basalt floor of intimate sales area
Photo credit: Sigurgeir Sigurjónsson

10

11

12

2

3

4

5

6

Ladies Fashion Shop
Athens, Greece
Anamorphosis Architects

Previous page:
Salon mirrors
2 Ceilings, multi-purpose lighting structure and display shelves
3 General view
4 Entrance ceiling and multi-purpose lighting structure
5 Salon, interior view
6 Reception area, panel system controlling outside view
Photo credit: courtesy Anamorphosis Architects

Marylebone Shop
London, UK
CD Partnership

1 First floor view of glass display
2 Main staircase

Photo credit: Peter Cook

Moschino
London, UK
Hosker Moore & Kent

3 Entrance; graphic symbols are inlaid into floor in black and white terrazzo
4&5 Ground floor view of 'Cheap & Chic' fashion collection
6 View of couture fitting room

Photo credit: courtesy Hosker Moore & Kent

1

2

3

4

5

6

2

3

4

5

Muji Shelton Street
London, UK
Harper Mackay Architects

Previous page:
View of changing room
2 Converted 2,200-square-foot Victorian warehouse in London's Covent Garden
3 Harper Mackay blend merchandise cohesively within raw exposed Victorian interior

Photo credit: Dennis Gilbert

Jigsaw Bond Street
London UK
John Pawson

4 Double stairs to basement
5 Double-height space

Photo credit: Richard Glover

Opticians Shop
Athens, Greece
Anamorphosis Architects

1 Staircase leading to mezzanine floor
2 Ground floor plan
3&4 Interior views
5 Entrance detail
6 Optics aluminium mirror-supporting element

Photo credit: courtesy Anamorphosis Architects

Tesco
London, UK
Michael Aukett Architects

7 View of shop interior

Photo credit: Dennis Gilbert

1

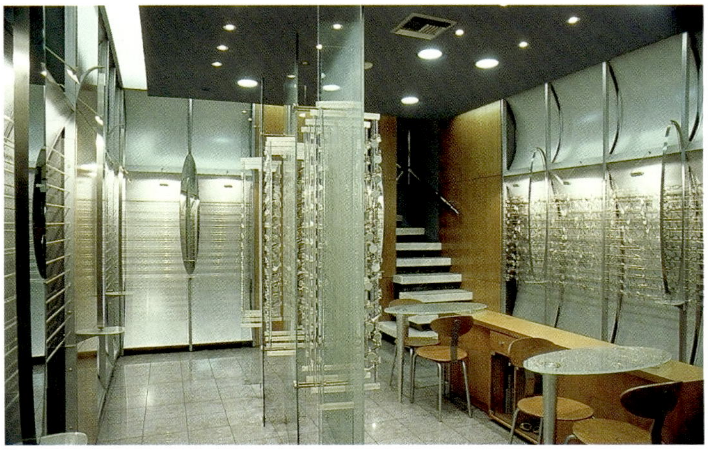

3

4

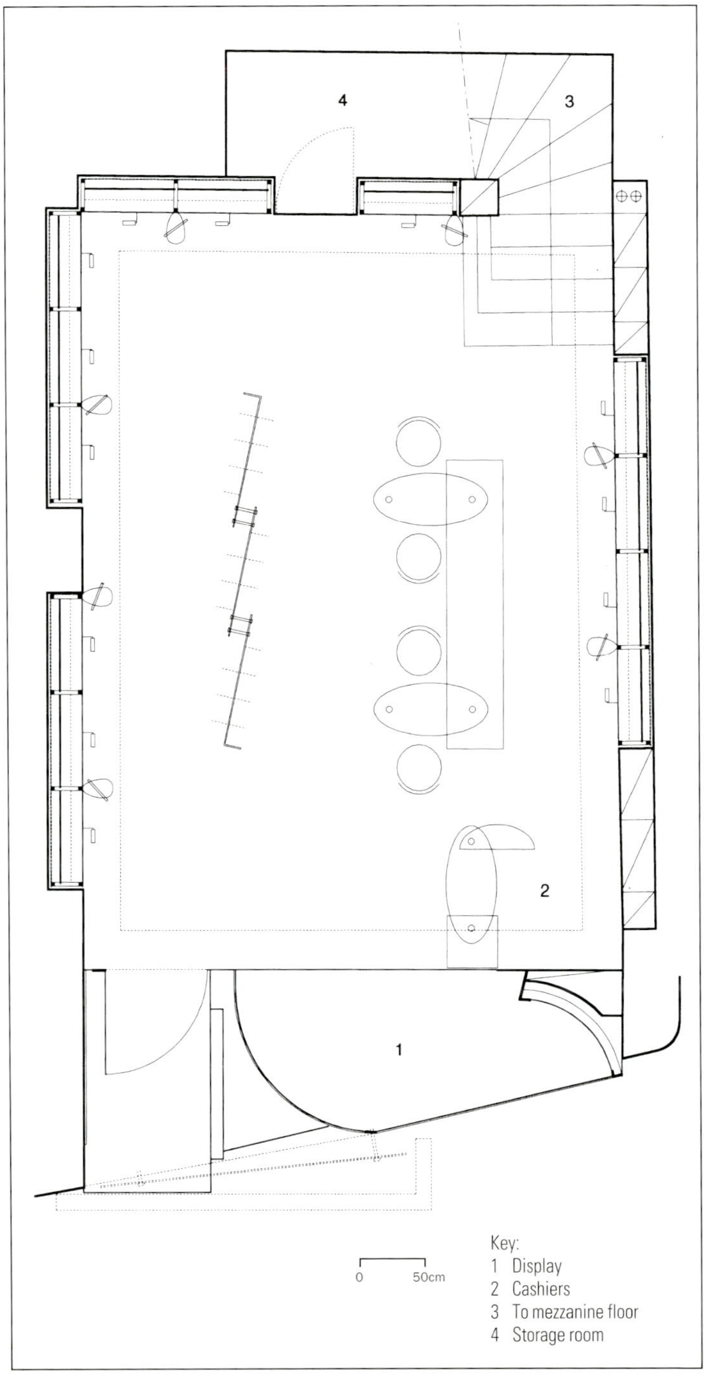

2

5

6

7

1

2

3

4

Valentino
Rome, Italy
Hosker Moore & Kent

1 Ground floor view at entrance
2 View of women's collection
3 Entrance view of staircase to first floor men's and women's collection
4 View down staircase back to entrance

Photo credit: courtesy Hosker Moore & Kent

5

6

7

Valentino
Sloane Street, London, UK
Hosker Moore & Kent

5 Ribbon staircase
6 View through staircase void
7 Top of staircase with view into women's wear
Photo credit: courtesy Hosker Moore & Kent

Biographies

Allford Hall Monoghan Morris Architects
London, UK

The firm's interest in architecture and approach to practice are indissoluble: building; teaching; writing; and, researching which all figure in their collective enthusiasm and act as a stimulus for their work.

Allford Hall Monoghan Morris's office has become a meeting point for clients, consultants and friends—a source of vital discussion beyond the terms of the partnership and indeed, the realm of architecture. As the firm has grown, a strong character has developed of its own in which all collaborators are vital, more for how they work together than for what they might achieve on their own. Ideas are encouraged to develop an autonomy from their author.

The diversity of work in the office has only furthered the firm's enthusiasm for investigation. Current projects include schemes for an art gallery, a school, a health centre, offices, a theatre, social housing, a bus station, even a construction site hoarding. This diversity has largely been won in specific building types.

Each project is seen to fulfil current needs, while being subject to strategic analysis of future requirements and talent opportunities. Simultaneously the firm's work looks to bridge the gulf between the traditions of its subject and the practicalities of the profession by reference to the world beyond and through the appropriation of familiar everyday objects and ideas. Around this process the firm identifies and defines the core ideas which the project strives to achieve.

The firm believes that the programme and the theoretical ideas which relate it to physical design are the most important generators of an architecture which is effective, popular and intellectually satisfying.

Austin-Smith:Lord
London, UK

With 50 years experience, Austin-Smith:Lord has earned a solid reputation for its creative approach to projects that require a blend of imagination and pragmatism. The base of the firm's design experience is broad and includes architecture, interior architecture, urban design and landscape.

The firm's reputation is further enhanced by its involvement in nationally recognized projects including historic preservation schemes, educational institutions, and judicial facilities.

Austin-Smith:Lord recognize the importance of place and context and therefore design buildings that respond to the environment. The firm's approach to planning and designing buildings and facilities means resolving its client's operational and service objectives within the context of the site. This approach seeks priority and order in the organization and operation of buildings, responding to the specifics of context with a form that is expressive in appearance, flexible in use and economic in construction. Innovative design creates buildings that are functional, attractive and generate wider benefits for both the user and the community as a whole.

Avery Associates
London, UK

Avery Associates is an innovative design-led practice well-known for its unique lateral thinking capabilities. This produces practical, unusual often unexpected, but always aesthetically elegant results, even in the most difficult of circumstances.

This approach has already been successfully applied to a wide variety of building types including commercial and residential buildings, arts and performance spaces, educational and university buildings, leisure, retail and museums. Perhaps the best known of these are the National Film Theatre and the Museum of the Moving Image (both part of London's South Bank Arts Centre), and No1 Neathouse Place—the reconstruction of a redundant 1960s London office block.

The practice has two major projects currently under construction: a large-screen IMAX cinema complex for the British Film Institute, valued at £11.5 million, and a new home for the Royal Academy of Dramatic Art, valued at £14.5 million.

In parallel with these major construction projects, Avery Associates has for many years been involved in research into new forms of habitation, new ways of using urban space, environmental initiatives such as the proposal for a national network of ecological beacons, and advanced construction materials and technologies. The firm has been fortunate to work with industry leaders such as Otis and British Steel and the practical benefits are seen in the application of these innovations to its built work.

The practice has an international reputation and its work has been published in North America, Europe, Scandinavia and Asia. Projects outside the United Kingdom include the European Teleport project for La Vaunage-Calvisson in France, a proposed master-plan for Abu Dhabi, and a planning study for the Helsinki-Tampere region in Finland.

The practice has won many prestigious awards, the most recent of which is the British Council for Offices 1998 award for Britain's Best Urban Workplace for the No1 Neathouse Place project.

Blauel Architects
London, UK

The practice was formed by Bernhard Blauel in 1986 and has since been joined by associates Andy Nettleton and Peter Jurschitzka. It has achieved a reputation for innovative projects which regularly receive press coverage. Designs for offices, private and public housing, cafés, banks and shops show an ability to carry out work in different national contexts. The successful design of the Cyberia Café at the Centre Pompidou in Paris led to further work on Internet Cafés including one recently completed in Bangkok. Other commissions include various contracts for the German Foreign Office, headquarters for two European banks and a corporate fit-out in the International Financial Centre (formerly NatWest Tower) in the City of London, fashion shops and offices in the West End of London, a contemporary gallery in Birmingham funded by the Arts Council and work for private clients in the UK, Germany, Italy and Switzerland.

The work demonstrates imaginative use of space and a concern for the most economical use of suitable materials combined with the application of modern building techniques. This approach has produced a light and airy architecture, whatever the size or circumstances, and has resulted in the practice being selected for the prestigious 40 under Forty exhibition at the Royal Institute of British Architects. Members of the practice engage in academic activity and the multi-national team of architects has contributed to a portfolio of work which is a synthesis of the best of continental European contemporary design and British architecture.

Fletcher Priest Architects
London, UK

Fletcher Priest Architects was established in 1978 by partners who had trained at the Architectural Association and worked together in a European design consultancy specializing in corporate identity. Since then, Fletcher Priest Architects has gained considerable experience in master-planning, architecture and interior design, developing a specialized knowledge of arts, cinema and office design.

Fletcher Priest Architects comprises 30 people in London and a further five in Köln. The offices are highly computerized enabling them to communicate with clients using 3-D rendered models and animations.

The practice has extensive experience working abroad with projects in Singapore, Tel Aviv, Stockholm, France, Holland, Germany, Ireland and the USA.

Fletcher Priest Architects has worked for international clients such as IBM, Sony, British Airways and WorldCom, and national UK organizations like the BBC, PowerGen, Howard De Walden Estates and the Corporation of London. The practice is currently designing the Vodafone Group's new headquarters complex at Newbury, UK; a major mixed-use development in Oxford Street, London; the 3-D IMAX cinema at London's Science Museum; digital TV and film post-production facilities for The Moving Picture Company, London; and production facilities for leading industrial companies.

Fletcher Priest Architects' work has been widely published and exhibited across Europe, and a number of projects have received awards for their design and operational qualities.

Foster and Partners
London, UK

Foster and Partners is an international architecture and design practice led by Sir Norman Foster and five partners—Spencer de Grey, David Nelson, Ken Shuttleworth, Graham Phillips, and Barry Cooke. Sir Norman Foster's philosophy of integration can be seen in the way the practice's London design studio works; it is essentially one large open space, shared equally by everyone, and free of subdivisions to encourage good communication between the many people who work there.

The practice's projects range in scale from Hong Kong's new airport—the largest construction project in the world—to its smallest commission, a door handle for Fusital. The scope of its work includes master-plans for cities, the design of buildings, interior design, product design, graphics and exhibitions. These can be found throughout the world, from the United Kingdom and Europe to the United States, Hong Kong, Japan, Saudi Arabia and Australia. Principal projects since the practice's inception in 1967 include: the Willis Faber and Dumas head office, Ipswich; the Sainsbury Centre for Visual Arts, Norwich; the Hongkong and Shanghai Banking Corporation Headquarters, Hong Kong; the Third London Airport, Stansted; the Carre d'Art, Nimes; the Commerzbank Headquarters, Frankfurt; the Great Court at the British Museum, London; the New German Parliament, Reichstag, Berlin; and the Millennium Bridge, London.

The central concern of the practice is design excellence, achieved through active collaboration with clients and specialists—from structural and environmental engineers to cost consultants. Cost management is of great importance—all projects have been built within their respective budgets, sometimes for considerably less—and many of the practice's award-winning projects have resulted from tough commercial circumstances. A wide range of supporting skills underpins the work of the practice, including model making, CAD drawing and visualization, and in-house audio-visual, photographic and printing systems.

Foster and Partners has received more than 160 awards and citations for design excellence, and won 50 national and international design competitions. Sir Norman Foster was appointed by the Queen to the Order of Merit as a Royal Designer for Industry, a Fellow of the Chartered Society of Designers, an Honorary Fellow of the Royal Academy of Engineering, and a Gold Medalist of both the Royal Institute of British Architects, and the American Institute of Architects. The practice has been awarded the Queen's Award for Export Achievement.

Jestico + Whiles Architects
London, UK

Jestico + Whiles Architects was formed in 1977 and now operates from its offices in Euston, London. It has associate offices in Prague, Munich, Riga, Sofia and Madrid.

The principals are Tom Jestico, John Whiles and Tony Ingram.

Industrial projects at Epsom (1979) and Waltham Cross (1982) employ lightweight structures and are technologically derived from automotive design. Bruges Place (1985), Hawgood Street (1986), Carlow Street (1990), and Burrell's Wharf (1988–1992), all in London, combine workspace, industrial use and housing to regenerate decayed urban areas, pioneering the move towards live/work units.

Social housing projects include Camden Gardens (1992), Arlington Road (1994), and Link Street (1998).

The practice has also designed prototype low-energy workspace for Friends of the Earth (1981 and 1986), the Policy Studies Institute (1986), Stukeley Street, London (1991), and Housing 21, Beaconsfield (1997). Following the re-building of The British Council, Prague (1993), the British Council, Madrid (1995), and the British Embassy, Riga, Latvia (1995), Jestico + Whiles has been commissioned to design the first zero-energy public building in the UK, for Hyndburn Borough Council (2000).

Jestico + Whiles Architects has now completed its second major hotel in London, One Aldwych (1998).

Paatela & Paatela, Architects Ltd.
Espoo, Finland

The name Paatela has been connected to healthcare architecture in Finland for 80 years. Founded in 1919 by Professor Jussi Paatela, the firm is now run by the third generation of the same family.

The largest healthcare institutions in Finland, such as Helsinki and Turku University Central Hospitals, have relied on the professional expertise of Paatela & Paatela, Architects Ltd throughout the years of practice. Today, the staff consists of several architects with over 20 years of experience in functional planning and architectural design of healthcare buildings. The projects have varied from large new hospital complexes to small renovations; and from municipal and district hospitals to private rehabilitation centres.

In addition to the healthcare sector, the firm has designed a variety of projects for research, education, corporate and industry sectors. In addition to larger projects, it has also been quite usual for the firm to design private houses and recreational buildings for its customers.

Besides complexes implemented in Finland, Paatela & Paatela, Architects Ltd. has designed projects in the Middle East, Africa, Russia and China.

Today, the firm utilizes the latest computer aided design methods to provide constantly up-to-date drawings and bills of quantities for each project.

Sergio Jaretti Sodano Architetto
Torino, Italy

Sergio Jaretti Architect has been involved in professional and cultural activities in Torino, Italy since 1955. His work spans many fields: architecture and building automation; interior and furniture design; urban and landscape design.

Every project is viewed as an interactive process involving its functions, design hypotheses and the need for checking and monitoring any changes that might occur while the project is in process. In this respect, the use of CAD is seen as essential.

Also deemed necessary within this philosophy is an awareness of the needs of future building occupants and the development of designs sympathetic with both the private and urban environments.

This philosophy was the impetus for Sergio Jaretti Architect founding the research society "Il Pensatoio" s.a.s. (The Thinktank) in 1983. This society publishes notebooks (*"Quaderni del Pensatoio"*) and organizes amongst other events, seminars and congresses.

Sergio Jaretti Archtiect's work includes the design and building of many residential homes, tourist resorts, and restoration work in universities, public hospitals and private dwelling restoration work.

Many of his works have been published in Italy and abroad in books and specialist magazines. He has also participated in several exhibitions in Italy (Rome, Torino, Milan and Bologna) and in other countries such as France, Germany, Switzerland, and Scandinavia.

STUDIOS Architecture
San Francisco, USA

Established in 1985, STUDIOS Architecture (STUDIOS), is a recognized industry leader with a world-wide reputation for excellence in architectural design. Providing services in strategic design, master-planning, architecture and interior architectural design, STUDIOS combines creative problem solving with a clear focus on the client's strategic objectives.

With offices in San Francisco, Washington DC, New York, Paris and London, STUDIOS has established a strong international presence with many projects completed and underway in Europe, Asia and the Middle East.

STUDIOS' clients include Silicon Graphics Computer Systems, 3Com Corporation, American Express, Morgan Stanley, Credit Suisse First Boston, Anderson Consulting, AirTouch Communications, MCI, Excite, and Young and Rubicam.

The firm has garnered more than 75 design awards and has been featured in more than 100 publications for its work around the world.

Index

Acknowledgments

IMAGES is pleased to add "Interior Spaces of Europe, Volume 2" to its compendium of design and architectural publications.

We wish to thank all participating firms for their valuable contribution to this publication and especially to Foster and Partners for providing the front cover image, and to Dennis Gilbert, the photographer.